# THE ZODIAC GUIDE TO

# VIRGO

ASTRID CARVEL

Red Wheel

This edition first published in 2024 by Red Wheel, an imprint of
Red Wheel/Weiser, LLC
With offices at:
65 Parker Street, Suite 7
Newburyport, MA 01950
www.redwheelweiser.com

ISBN: 978-1-59003-546-7

Printed and bound in China
1010 Printing International Ltd
10  9  8  7  6  5  4  3  2  1

# Contents

# Introduction

Are you ready to open your mind to the ancient wisdom of the zodiac and explore the possibilities contained within? Astrology is as far-reaching as the night sky itself, an intricate web of stars, constellations, planets, celestial spheres and horizons, mapped out by ancient cultures in millennia gone by in an attempt to make sense of our time on Earth.

This book will equip you with the tools you need to explore more deeply your behaviors, characteristics and connections; to open up the possibilities held in the movement of the planets, and help you to find guidance and comfort when you need it.

Astrology is a voyage of self-discovery, into which you can dip or dive as you wish, taking on a few morsels from the stars or getting stuck in to the complexities held within.

Among these pages you'll find a wealth of insight into the history of the zodiac and the different astrological traditions. You'll learn how to build your own birth chart, what it all means and what you can gain from it.

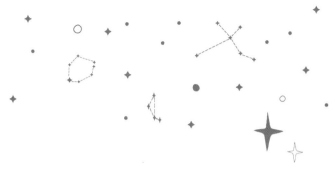

You'll look at how the position of the planets contain meaning, how to decipher your sun, moon and rising signs, and more. You'll look at the houses – the segments of the sky that relate to different aspects of your life – and how to decode their teachings. The patterns created by celestial matter across the houses are decoded here in order for you to easily digest what it all means.

Then you'll move on to the details of your sun sign and how it relates to all areas of your existence, as well as the self-care practices you can benefit from, with ideas and suggestions specific to your sign of the zodiac.

So, what are you waiting for? Turn the page and let the journey begin.

# Part 1

## WELCOME TO THE ZODIAC

This chapter will take you on a journey through the birth of the zodiac, thousands of years ago, to its relevance in modern times. To understand your sun sign – often referred to as your zodiac or star sign – you might first want to delve into the history and traditions that led to the widely practiced movement that is known today. What moved people to look to the sky for guidance long ago and why do people still do it? Research suggests that today astrology is more popular than ever. It has experienced something of a resurgence, perhaps because the myriad uncertainties of life push people towards the darkness above in search of comfort. The far-reaching knowledge of the stars is yours for the taking – are you ready?

# What is astrology?

Before you go any further, it's important to differentiate between astronomy and astrology. **Astronomy** is the scientific study of the universe, including planets, stars, celestial objects and space itself. **Astrology** looks at how the position of the stars and planets at the time of our birth can affect our personality and shape how we live our lives.

While astrology is an interpretation of the position of the planets and stars, it relates closely to human behavior and the influence of celestial bodies on our everyday choices, moods and behavior. Astrologers believe that everything is part of an interconnected reality and that understanding how the ancient symbolism of the stars and planets can relate to events in your own life is a constantly evolving process.

While astrology does not suppose that the planets and stars control you, nor does it predict the future, it does suggest that the celestial sphere is able to create certain conditions and situations that you can learn to use to your advantage. It might take practice, but the potential in the stars is there for the taking.

Horoscopes in magazines and newspapers are just the tip of the iceberg. To find out what makes you tick from an astrological perspective you simply need to know your birth date. From there you can uncover your sun, moon and rising signs, create a birth chart and learn more about yourself. We'll get to those later. The world of astrology is far-reaching and open to all, and can help you to understand your foibles, behaviors and relationships. It can help you decode your past and open your mind to the future.

The first step on your celestial path is a crucial one – it's time to learn about the zodiac.

# History of the zodiac

Long before people could travel into space – or even before telescopes allowed us to study worlds beyond ours in more detail – humans gazed up at the night sky to keep track of the time of year and planned their lives around the position of the stars. Many a traveller has looked to the sky to determine which route to take, with ancient sailors putting their trust in the celestial map and using the North Star for guidance. In ancient Egypt farmers were prewarned of the annual Nile flood in July by the rising of Sirius, the Dog Star. The Phoenicians assessed the Sun's position in the heavens when they needed to know which direction to take, and a lunar calendar led by the phases of the moon was drawn up by ancient cultures to keep track of religious events.

While it's something of a mystery when exactly the signs of the zodiac became linked to human characteristics and behaviors, we do know that they originated as a time-measuring device. By mapping out the constellations in a strip of the sky spanning the circumference of the Earth – in which the Sun, Moon and planets moved – and dividing that strip into 12 segments, early astrologers were able to create a calendar of zodiac signs.

The sky is divided into 12 segments and each is occupied by a zodiac sign. Each sign is represented by a constellation that loosely outlines the symbol attached to that sign, and it takes approximately one month for the Sun to travel through each sign's segment. This is the reason that in astrology the signs of the zodiac are known as Sun signs.

While the Ancient Greeks are largely thought to be responsible for devising the Zodiac calendar we are familiar with today, there is evidence of the Babylonians living by a similar set of signs as far back as 1500 BCE.

### Why does the zodiac calendar start in March?

The Ancient Greeks believed the first day of spring occurred when the sun appeared in the constellation Aries, marking the beginning of the calendar. It made sense for the year to start with the green shoots emerging after winter, with spring signifying new beginnings.

# *How it works*

There are myriad techniques and applications when it comes to astrology, but the most widely used in the West today is modern or psychological astrology (see page 28).

Before you do anything else, you need to create your birth chart. In the modern age, this can be done quite easily using the internet, however before the technological age those in search of answers in the stars had to search great reams of dusty pages to find the information they needed to compile their trusted chart.

Your birth chart maps out the position of the key stars and planets in the sky on the day you were born. This chart is the basis for every horoscope or reading you might have. An astrologer – or you once you get the hang of it – compares your birth chart with the position of the planets and stars at key moments to understand your motivations. Knowing how the planets behave allows for predictions about an individual's behavior to be gauged in certain situations and at a certain time. None of this is a given, but many find comfort in being granted an insight into their psyche.

Combining the planetary movements with inform-ation about your sun or zodiac sign, along with your moon and rising signs (see pages 76–81), as well as your element (see page 24) you can gather more information about what really makes you tick and even understand why certain characteristics of your personality differ from those of other people in your life.

Throughout this book you'll learn about the different aspects of astrology that allow you to access a clearer picture of yourself.

# Useful terms

**Zodiac** – this is a band across the sky through which the Sun, Moon and visible planets move throughout the year. The zodiac is divided into 12 segments according to the constellations that represent the 12 sun signs – Aries, Taurus, Gemini, Cancer, Leo, Virgo, Libra, Scorpio, Sagittarius, Capricorn, Aquarius and Pisces.

**Sun sign** – this is your sign in the zodiac, relating to when you were born; for example, if you were born on 21 April your sun sign would be Taurus.

**Birth chart** – a birth chart is a snapshot of the position of the planets on the day you were born.

**Planets** – in astrology the planets refer to those in the solar system – Mercury, Venus, Mars, Jupiter, Saturn, Neptune and Pluto (despite this being declassified in more recent times). The Sun and Moon are also considered planets in modern astrology.

**Houses** – 12 segments of the night sky that overlap the signs of the zodiac. Each house reflects a different area of your life.

**Elements** – each sun sign is assigned one of four elements – fire, water, air or earth.

**Moon sign** – your moon sign is the sign of the zodiac where the Moon was positioned on the day of your birth.

**Rising sign** – your rising sign is the sign of the zodiac that was rising (or ascending) on the eastern horizon on the day of your birth.

**Retrograde** – this refers to an optical illusion that makes it look like the planets are moving backwards, due to their movement through the night sky relative to the Earth.

**Midpoint** – a midpoint is the measured halfway point between two celestial objects on your chart.

**Horoscope** – your horoscope is an astrological map of the positions of the Sun, Moon and planets at a given moment in time in relation to your sun, moon and rising signs. This map can be used to help understand past events or hint towards future ones.

# *Your sun sign*

Sun signs are simply another way of referring to star or zodiac signs. With the Earth making one full revolution of the Sun per year, it spends around one month in each of the 12 zodiac signs. Your sun sign is determined by your birth date: whichever sign – be that Aries, Taurus, Gemini, Cancer, Leo, Virgo, Libra, Scorpio, Sagittarius, Capricorn, Aquarius or Pisces – the Sun was transiting through at the time you were born is that which is astrologically assigned to you.

It is impossible to be a "pure" Aries, for example, because all of the other planets would have to be positioned in your sign's segment of the sky at the time of your birth, which due to their orbits and distance from each other could never happen. With the Sun considered the most influential of the celestial objects in your horoscope, your sun sign is believed to be a valuable source from which to learn a great deal about yourself.

However, in order to gain a complete picture of yourself, you must analyse the Sun's influence alongside that of the other planets in your horoscope – the most important being your rising and moon signs. If you

don't yet know your signs, you'll learn how to determine these on the following pages. These vital elements of your birth chart (see page 70) help to uncover cosmic insights into your character and inner workings.

## How to calculate your sun sign

Working out your sun sign is simple. Check the list below for the sign that falls on your birthday.

| Aries | – | 21 March–20 April |
| Taurus | – | 21 April–21 May |
| Gemini | – | 22 May–21 June |
| Cancer | – | 22 June–22 July |
| Leo | – | 23 July–23 August |
| Virgo | – | 24 August–22 September |
| Libra | – | 23 September–23 October |
| Scorpio | – | 24 October–22 November |
| Sagittarius | – | 23 November–21 December |
| Capricorn | – | 22 December–20 January |
| Aquarius | – | 21 January–18 February |
| Pisces | – | 19 February–20 March |

# *The signs*

## ARIES *(21 March–20 April)*

**Symbol: Ram**
**Element: Fire**
**Ruling planet: Mars**

Aries people are brave and headstrong, but can also be childish, impatient and impulsive. They are determined and direct, able to be both straightforward and clear-headed when making decisions. Aries people are natural born leaders and, much like their animal counterpart the ram, they are fiercely independent. They are very passionate thrill-seekers with a zest for life.

## TAURUS *(21 April–21 May)*

**Symbol: Bull**
**Element: Earth**
**Ruling planet: Venus**

Taurus people are patient and dependable, persevering to the very end. They show untold loyalty to family and friends, and their quiet strength and determination is an inspiration to others. A Taurus is not a fan of change and does not like being rushed. They long for stability and home comforts. In relationships, Tauruses look for emotional security – they may take their time looking for it, but when they find it, they work hard to hold on to it.

## GEMINI *(22 May–21 June)*

**Symbol: Twin**
**Element: Air**
**Ruling planet: Mercury**

Geminis are cheerful and upbeat people, while also being curious and rational. They are good communicators and are incredibly sociable, often keen to engage with anyone and everyone they meet. A Gemini's twin element sees two sides to their personality, and they also have a fickle and superficial nature that they need to work to control. They seek a lively rapport in relationships and have a knack of finding something in common with everyone.

## CANCER *(22 June–22 July)*

**Symbol: Crab**
**Element: Water**
**Ruling planet: the Moon**

Cancerians are caring souls who are immensely protective of their friends and loved ones. Much like that of their animal counterpart, the crab, they project a tough, shell-like exterior to conceal their sensitivity. Headstrong and stubborn, it can be difficult to convince a Cancerian to give something up when they have it in their sights. They can also be argumentative, but an overriding kindness runs deep with this sign.

## LEO *(23 July–23 August)*

**Symbol: Lion**
**Element: Fire**
**Ruling planet: the Sun**

Leos are attention-seekers who bring energy to those around them. They love nothing more than to have an adoring audience and are proud of their flamboyance. A Leo excels in both creativity and organization, and can be quick to impress this on others whose lives are more chaotic – sometimes without invitation. Leos are often the more dominant in relationships, but bring kindness, warmth and generosity with them.

## VIRGO *(24 August–22 September)*

**Symbol: Maiden**
**Element: Earth**
**Ruling planet: Mercury**

Virgos are constantly on the go, busier than all the other signs and in constant pursuit of perfection. Practical, organized and thoughtful people, Virgos are always willing to offer assistance or advice and will help whenever they can. While kind and patient in relationships, a Virgo can also require reassurance to boost their confidence and relax into their situation.

## LIBRA *(23 September–23 October)*

**Symbol: Scales**
**Element: Air**
**Ruling planet: Venus**

Libras use their skills of diplomacy to strive for peace and harmony in all areas of their lives. When it comes to decision-making, they can ruminate at length and often seek the advice of others for guidance. These charming individuals tend to shy away from high-pressure situations in order to find a happier balance. A Libra is both romantic and generous when it comes to relationships, however they harbor high expectations in love.

## SCORPIO *(24 October–22 November)*

**Symbol: Scorpion**
**Element: Water**
**Ruling planet: Pluto**

Scorpio is one of the more emotional signs of the zodiac, with jealousy an overriding theme that they work hard to contain. However, combined with strong willpower, this can often drive them to reach for their goals. With boundless energy, Scorpios are often high achievers, and their knack for deep, analytical thought pushes them to get to the root of problems. In relationships, when a Scorpio sets their sights on someone, they do all they can to get what they want – and are fiercely loyal.

## SAGITTARIUS *(23 November–21 December)*

**Symbol: Archer**
**Element: Fire**
**Ruling planet: Jupiter**

Sagittarians are thrill-seekers who are always up for a challenge and in pursuit of adventure. Their enthusiasm and optimism can be infectious, leading them to be popular among others who often enjoy their company and zest for life. In relationships, Sagittarians don't like to be restricted, and their independent spirit and restlessness can lead them to grow bored easily, needing romantic situations to remain fresh and exciting.

## CAPRICORN *(22 December–20 January)*

**Symbol: Goat**
**Element: Earth**
**Ruling planet: Saturn**

Capricorns are realistic and carefully approach situations in a logical manner. Slow and steady wins the race with this sign – with Capricorns quietly moving towards the prize with composure and without haste. A unique sense of humor is a key trait of a Capricorn and, when it comes to relationships, they are both loyal and devoted.

## AQUARIUS *(21 January–18 February)*

**Symbol: Water-bearer**
**Element: Air**
**Ruling planet: Uranus**

Aquarians are often glamourous, eccentric people, always friendly and often overly helpful. They are genuinely curious about everyone they meet and will quiz them at great length about their lives, however they tend to shroud their own in mystery. In relationships Aquarians are independent and need their space, which can make it hard to settle down.

## PISCES *(19 February–20 March)*

**Symbol: Fish**
**Element: Water**
**Ruling planet: Neptune**

Pisceans are kind people, often going out of their way to be both friendly and charitable. This gentle sign promotes compassion and understanding, and a Pisces is not afraid to wear their heart on their sleeve – opening up and sharing their feelings with those they care for. In relationships Pisceans can be overly affectionate and often keep their emotions close to the surface.

# *The elements*

The 12 sun signs are split into four groups, with each represented by an element. Traditionalists believe these vital elements make up the entire universe. Fire, air, water and earth are regarded as the four basic principles of life, in turn corresponding to four basic principles of the psyche. Knowing our element sign allows us to probe further into the characteristics associated with it.

## FIRE

**Fire signs: Aries, Leo, Sagittarius**
Fire signs are bright and sparky, artistic and passionate. You can expect them to be confident in their independence and never afraid to speak up. Ever the optimists, fire signs make things happen and don't mind the pressure that might come along with it.

## AIR

**Air signs: Libra, Aquarius, Gemini**
Air signs are social creatures, they know how to work the room and offer engaging conversation. While equally witty and entertaining, they are also good listeners and know when to offer a sympathetic ear to others.

## WATER

**Water signs: Cancer, Scorpio, Pisces**

Water signs are in touch with their emotions, and are both empathetic and nurturing to others. Always ready to offer help, they will step up when they are needed. Water signs are imaginative and can be quiet thinkers.

## EARTH

**Earth signs: Capricorn, Taurus, Virgo**

Earth signs are all about the details. While they are practical and grounded, they look to the future and start building for it way ahead of time. Earth signs are down-to-earth people and are often called the "gardeners of the zodiac", in part due to the care and attention they pay their family and friends.

### The fifth element

Some Western sources believe in a fifth element known as the *quinta essentia* – or simply, "spirit". This element is frequently overlooked because it describes the soul or spiritual being of someone and stands apart from the other four elements. While some astrological applications take the fifth element into account when analyzing signs, it is not depicted in the horoscope.

# Different astrological traditions

Over the centuries, different cultures around the world have developed their own astrological traditions and systems. It's fascinating to see how these differ and how they all came about.

## WESTERN

In the West, the most commonly used astrological system is derived from the ancient form of astrology based on the 12 signs of the zodiac. This system spans popular culture in its basic form of sun sign horoscopes focusing on human behavior and motivation, and is led by the 12 constellations attached to the 12 sun signs.

## MAYAN

Mayan astrology is based on an ancient and complex calendar known as the Tzolk'in, which consists of 20 day signs and 13 galactic numbers. The 260-day calendar is often used to suggest future events and identify different human characteristics. Instead of elements, the Mayan astrological system uses directions – north, east, south, west – which each carry a different set of meanings and a direction is assigned to each of the 20 day signs.

## VEDIC

Vedic – or jyotish – astrology is derived from ancient Indian traditions and is one of the oldest and most-practiced forms of astrology in the East. While the vedic and Western zodiac follow pretty much the same 12 signs, the dates are different – for example, Aries runs from 13 April–14 May, while Taurus sits between 15 May–14 June (as opposed to 21 March–20 April for Aries and 21 April–21 May for Taurus in the Western calendar). This is because it is based on the fixed, observable positions of the related constellations, whereas Western astrology takes into account the shifting of the Earth on its axis over millennia and is instead based on the changeable position of the sun.

## CHINESE

This system is based on the lunar cycles and the power of five elements – wood, fire, earth, metal and water. Drawing from ancient Chinese philosophy, and the concept of yin and yang, each year is associated with an animal as well as an element.

# *Different astrological techniques*

There are many different astrological practices, but the ones outlined below are some of the most widely used across the world.

## MODERN ASTROLOGY

Also referred to as "psychological astrology", this is the most popular type of astrology in the West and is the technique that will be the focus of this book. It is a practice with many layers, but in simple terms, modern astrology looks at the position of the planets in relation to your birth chart – which is a snapshot of the planets and stars on the day you were born – and uses the information to understand your personality, characteristics and behaviors.

Alan Leo was a respected British astrologer who revived the practice in the late 1800s and early 1900s, following its fall from favor at the end of the 1600s. Leo – who used his sun sign as a pseudonym – is widely referred to as the "father of modern astrology", thanks to the way he helped to move it away from fortune-telling and encouraged people to use it to explore behavior and personality through a psychological lens.

## HORARY

The Horary astrology technique is rooted in ancient Hellenistic traditions and seeks to answer a question by creating a horoscope for the moment the question is asked. The astrologer will generally receive a simple "yes" or "no" answer to the question being posed.

## MUNDANE

Mundane astrology studies the effect of the planets on groups of people, places and countries. This branch of astrology focuses on significant events throughout history and looks to understand it through the creation of a birth chart for that moment in time. A horoscope can then be created for that event to explain how people might react to or cope with such an event.

## ELECTIVE

Elective astrology looks at the optimal time for an event to occur, based on the position of the planets. An astrologer might advise you to get married at a time when Venus – the planet of love and harmony – is aligned with the planet's position on your own birth chart, for example.

## RELATIONSHIP

This branch of astrology looks at how compatible two individuals are likely to be in love. An astrologer will study the birth charts of the two individuals to see how well they will get along. There are two ways of doing this. The first is synastry, which compares the two birth charts side by side; and the second is composite, which involves calculating the midpoints of the planets on each person's birth chart to create a new chart for the pairing, which is then interpreted afresh.

## TRADITIONAL

Until the twentieth century and the introduction of modern astrology, most branches of the practice were considered "traditional". This form is all about prediction and only uses the seven "planets" we can see with the naked eye to do so, namely the Sun, Moon, Mercury, Venus, Mars, Jupiter and Saturn.

## LOCATIONAL

Locational astrology looks at a birth chart to determine where the bearer should exist or spend time. According to the position of certain planets in relation to the subject's own, they can advise where they should live or go on holiday. If someone wanted to know where

they were likely to have the most successful holiday, for example, an astrologer might look at the position of Venus (representing enjoyment) and Jupiter (long-distance travel) in order to deduce the ideal location. This is also known as "astro-mapping".

## MEDICAL

Medical astrology is all about the health of a person, whereby an astrologer uses an individual's birth chart to discover the cause of any health issues they may have. The health problem, cures and area or areas of the body in which it occurs all correspond to specific planetary positions.

### Science fiction?

Modern astrology is more popular than ever, with younger generations increasingly adopting the practice in an attempt to understand their own lives. And they hold it in high esteem: a National Science Foundation poll conducted in recent years found that more than half of millennials believe astrology to be a science.

# *What astrology can do for you*

Astrology does not predict your future or describe your personality in certain terms; instead it describes the potential for particular characteristics or events to come to light. Astrology can help you know what you are capable of as a human being, and when to take advantage of challenging or opportunistic times. Astrology does not negate your own free will – you are not controlled by the planets – but the planets do create certain atmospheres and conditions that you can learn to use to your advantage.

When you understand why you act in a certain way or acknowledge your fears and desires, you feel more at ease with yourself and your world. When you know yourself better you act with conscious awareness of what you're doing and why.

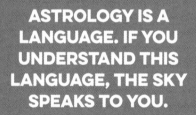

**ASTROLOGY IS A LANGUAGE. IF YOU UNDERSTAND THIS LANGUAGE, THE SKY SPEAKS TO YOU.**

DANE RUDHYAR

# *Part 2*

## MEET VIRGO

---

As the sixth sign of the zodiac, Virgo is a high achiever. You really push yourself to the best of your abilities and are incredibly productive with it. You are a kind-hearted soul, thoughtful and trustworthy, and are able to keep calm in a crisis. Virgos make great friends. You are ever reliable and present, able to pick up the pieces when things fall apart. You are also unflinchingly honest, straight to the point and able to swiftly take charge of a situation. You tell it like it is and then get on with it. Your need for control can sometimes be overbearing, but if you rein this in, all will work out in the end. Over the following pages we'll take a more detailed look at what really makes you tick in all areas of life, from career to wealth, love and romance, relationships with friends and family, health and well-being, and compatible signs. We'll find out what the planets mean to you, as well as your strengths and challenges.

# Factfile: Virgo

**DATES:** 24 August–22 September

**REPRESENTATION:** Virgin

**SYMBOL:** ♍

**CHARACTER TRAITS:** Capable, perfectionist, efficient

**BODY PART:** Intestines

**ELEMENT:** Earth

**RULING PLANET:** Mercury

**COLOR:** Brown

**BIRTHSTONE:** Peridot (August), sapphire (September)

**ASSOCIATED CRYSTALS:** Amazonite, amethyst, fluorite

**CHAKRA:** Throat

## TRIVIA

+ Virgo is the sixth sign of the zodiac, after Leo and before Libra. It is the second of the earth signs, the others being Taurus and Capricorn.

+ The word "Virgo" means "virgin" in Latin and the symbol for the constellation is a young woman.

+ Representing fertility and agriculture, Virgo is visible in the northern hemisphere in the spring and summer months, and the southern hemisphere in autumn and winter.

+ The constellation of Virgo's brightest star is Spica, a bright blue-white star, which can be located by following the curve of the handle of the Big Dipper (also known as the Plough) to the next two bright stars – Spica is the second of these.

+ Spica is almost twice as big as the Sun and is situated 260 light years from Earth.

+ Other stars of note include the second brightest Gamma Virginis, a binary star, and the third brightest Epsilon Virginis, a giant, yellow star also known as "the grape gatherer".

# The history of Virgo

In Greek mythology, Virgo is related to several different stories.

The first is that of Astraea, virgin goddess of justice, and daughter of Zeus and Themis. Astraea represents natural law and upholds the balance of the seasons. During the Golden Age, Astraea lived on Earth among mortals, but with the dawn of the Bronze Age came lawlessness she could not abide. Astraea was driven away from Earth and Zeus set her among the stars to become the constellation Virgo. According to the myth Astraea will return to Earth when the Golden Age comes again.

Another tale related to Virgo is the tragic Greek myth of Erigone, daughter of Icarius of Attica. The story goes that Icarius was murdered and his body buried. Worried what might have become of her missing father, Erigone took her dog and went out to look for him. When the dog found her father's shallow grave, Erigone was incensed with grief and hanged herself from a nearby tree.

God of fertility and wine Dionysus took pity on the tragic father and daughter figures, and sent them up to be together again in the sky – Icarius as the constellation Boötes and Erigone as Virgo.

# Virgo:
## what the planets tell us

One of the most important strands of astrology is what the planets can tell us when they are transitioning through your sun sign. You can find planetary transition predictions on various websites including this one: astrosage.com/transits. Note: as outer and therefore slower-moving planets, Uranus, Neptune and Pluto take hundreds of years to move through all 12 signs of the zodiac! Therefore what they can tell us is far broader and less personal.

**The Sun: purpose** – You spend your life developing a skill, something practical that you can use in your work life.

**The Moon: instinct** – You offer logical advice when people come to you and are protective over others. When it comes to looking after yourself, you focus on exercise and diet.

**Mercury: communication** – You are quite analytical and good with numbers. You're able to sort data in a way that makes others envious.

**Venus: love** – You show your partner you love them through small, everyday gestures. You are affectionate and romantic.

**Mars: action** – You are a maker and a fixer, keen to work with your hands creatively; you also make do and repair as needed.

**Jupiter: opportunity** – If you keep an eye on the details, you will reap the rewards. Find joy in your work and charitable pursuits.

**Saturn: authority** – You have what it takes to rise to the top in your chosen field, so put your talents to good use.

**Uranus: change** – Uranus represents sudden change and innovation, as well as the advancing of science and technology.

**Neptune: imagination** – As well as intuition, glamour and enchantment, Neptune moves us to ask ourselves important questions in the quest for another path.

**Pluto: power** – Pluto is about the bigger picture and not worrying about the small stuff. Due to its incredibly slow orbit, it can take between 12 and 30 years for Pluto to move through one sign – and a whopping 248 years to transition through the whole zodiac. This is why Pluto is known as "the generational planet", with whole generations finding Pluto on their birth chart.

## 2060 Chiron

Some branches of astrology also include 2060 Chiron, a minor planet in the outer solar system orbiting the sun between Saturn and Uranus. Discovered in 1977, it suggests that self-assurance will promote healing as you look to find independence from your situation.

# *Virgo: personality traits and characteristics*

Often called the healer of the zodiac, Virgos like to take charge of situations and make things right. You are kind and thoughtful with others, not just keen to help a little, but to problem-solve them out of their unfortunate circumstances. You are cool and collected, which can certainly be a bonus when others are losing their heads. Your logical brain and attention to detail go a long way to offer advice to others and help them come up with options.

This, of course, helps you to navigate your own life too and retain control over it – but be prepared to sometimes lose control and learn to accept when things are out of your hands. Virgos can find this very challenging and the lack of control over people or situations can lead to a spike in anxiety. Offset this with short sessions of guided meditation or with a high-energy workout to give your brain a boost.

You are a hard worker and meticulous when trusted with a task. You're also likely to be a bit of an overachiever, whether at work, play or life in general. You're incredibly productive and just get the job done, whatever it may be. You get on with things without any fuss and for this reason are the first call when someone needs a job done properly – either at work or home, with friends or family.

## Virgo: strengths and challenges

### STRENGTHS

✦ You are calm in a crisis, which is incredibly valuable in many areas of life. Friends and family know they can rely on you to be coolheaded and to come up with practical solutions when things go south.

✦ You are a no-nonsense sort of person, straight to the point and to the finish line of any task, project or situation. You don't like a fuss, but you also don't make one. People look to you as a natural leader and someone who leaves no stone unturned.

✦ Kindness shines out of your pores and you are unbelievably thoughtful. Whether big or small gestures, you remember things that others so easily forget, and people in your life love you for it.

## CHALLENGES

✦ You are a perfectionist, a bit of a control freak, and it can be incredibly beneficial to learn to let go of that control and allow more spontaneity into your life. Start by leaving a weekend wide open in your diary – don't make any plans and just see where the wind takes you.

✦ You can be overly analytical, and can see those on the receiving end turn a little frosty. Be careful not to give others a hard time, and tune back in to your kind and thoughtful side.

✦ You're not the best at handling change and would prefer it if everything stayed just as it was. This isn't a realistic way to go about life; we all experience change at some point, whether small or life-altering, and we owe it to ourselves to learn to cope with the small changes so we can handle the big ones when they arise.

## Virgo: interests, likes and dislikes

### INTERESTS

You love things that flex your mind, so reading is high on the agenda – and you'll read anything from fiction to non-fiction books, magazines, newspapers and blogs. You're the type to read the newspaper from cover to cover on the weekend and are always up on current world events.

Games that challenge you, such as chess and board games involving letters, words and trivia, are right up your alley. You are a competitive soul and get engrossed when the board games come out.

### LIKES

There's nothing you like more than a good debate with friends, family, acquaintances or colleagues – whoever is up for it! The topic doesn't matter, whatever it is it's likely you have read up on it, have an opinion about it and can argue it extremely effectively.

Your kind heart means you like to help others. You're one of the first to volunteer your time when you have some to spare – whether that's to help charitable causes or friends who are struggling.

You like a clean home and will spend a good amount of time to ensure it is free of dust, dirt and clutter. Your pristine home is the envy of friends and family, and you're often the one volunteering to help them clear the clutter and get their home in order.

## DISLIKES

You don't like it when you're not in control. Delayed trains and bad traffic drive you up the wall. Try taking a deep breath in these situations and remind yourself it's out of your hands.

Feeling vulnerable is a no-no for you. You don't like others to see your weaknesses, and prefer instead to be seen as a strong and capable person able to tackle any challenge head on.

# *Virgo: communication style*

Virgos tell it like it is – there's no messing around with this sign. Your no-nonsense attitude is apparent in the way you communicate with others and although you are most definitely a kind soul, you certainly don't put up with any nonsense. Perhaps that's why you're so good at helping others when they're having to deal with their own.

You are trusted by those who know you well and usually by those who only know you a little. Your honesty helps. People know they will get the truth when they ask for your opinion or for life advice.

Your worldly knowledge means you have an answer for almost everything, which is why you are so good at debating your favored point of view.

You're the one pouring "just one more" drink at the end of the night at dinner parties, because there's always more left to talk about. You're clever and you're witty with it, which makes others relaxed and charmed by your company.

While you generally ooze confidence when you speak and are able to get your point across clearly, certain anxieties can lurk underneath. If someone throws you a curveball mid-discussion, especially in a work situation, you might find yourself caught off guard and vulnerable.

# Virgo: compatibility with other signs

Remember this is not hard and fast – the zodiac moves in mysterious ways and just because your sign might appear incompatible with that of someone you are close to doesn't mean a friendship or more is off the table. As always, the zodiac is just a guide.

**Aries** – These two are a challenging combination, however Virgo is attracted to Aries' passion for many things and Aries appreciates Virgo's practical nature.

**Taurus** – Virgo can grow frustrated by Taurus' indecision, however both love the natural world and are excited to have someone to share it with.

**Gemini** – Curious, highly sociable and detail-oriented, Virgo and Gemini are very similar on many levels, and can make an exceptional pairing.

**Cancer** – Cancer and Virgo excite each other, with Cancer attracted to Virgo's logical, practical approach, and Virgo won over by Cancer's nurturing tendencies.

**Leo** – Virgo and Leo get along extremely well and share a similar sense of humor, but when they fight, they really fight. Luckily, they're good at making up.

**Virgo** – Two straightforward people in a relationship can mean there are no hidden agendas and each one is an open book to the other – however, both have very high standards.

**Libra** – Libra and Virgo can find themselves locking horns if they're not careful, but they can also learn a lot from each other.

**Scorpio** – These two are fairly in awe of each other; add to that the intensity in the bedroom and there are sparks flying everywhere.

**Sagittarius** – Virgo and Sagittarius have a lot of respect for each other and a lot in common: they both love reading, traveling and adventure.

**Capricorn** – These two are both so busy they barely have time for each other. Neither is able to make the other take a break when they need.

**Aquarius** – Both hard workers, Virgo and Aquarius have much in common and a mutual respect for each other. These two signs can learn much from one another.

**Pisces** – A positive pairing of two signs that – while they bring different skills to the partnership – are both all about honesty and truth.

# Virgo: relationships – friends and family

Virgos make trusted and supportive friends, and have the ability to really make others feel special. Your kind and thoughtful nature are to the fore as a friend and relation, and you're the first to lend a hand when it is needed. Your frank take on things, too, is greatly appreciated by those who seek your advice.

You're keen to spend time with your family when you can and, ever helpful, you're the one doing favors and chores for older relatives, and no doubt ferrying around younger ones. You're the family cornerstone who gets everyone together – a reliable presence guaranteed to fix a sticky situation, should it arise.

Be wary of being overly involved in your relatives' lives and notice when you need to take a step back and give them some privacy. Your controlling nature can mean your patience is liable to wane around relatives in constant need of help as you become overly critical about their life choices. Take a moment to put yourself in their shoes and think about how the situation feels for them.

Similarly, when it comes to your parenting style, you can be overly involved in your children's lives too. Be present, be encouraging, but let them make decisions on their own and have their space when they need it.

# *Virgo:*
# *love and sex*

While Virgo has confidence in abundance at work, in relationships this can be less apparent. You might find yourself needing reassurance in relationships, often asking yourself what your partner sees in you and whether they're going to end it all over a minor argument.

It's important to you that your partner is someone who is able to tell you fairly regularly that you are important to them and the reasons why they care for you. Be wary of becoming overly needy and try some positive affirmations in the mirror to help build your confidence (see page 105).

Your love of control and organization means you like routine in a relationship.

You like to know when you're going to be spending time with your partner and will be the first to suggest a shared calendar so you can schedule your commitments around each other.

The bedroom is one of the few places where you like to lose control, really let go and enjoy yourself. This is the place where you love spontaneity from your partner. A sensual massage can really help you to relax, get in the mood and forget about your mile-long to-do list.

# Virgo: career and success

One of the zodiac's great achievers, Virgos are as productive as they come. When you start a project, you don't waver until you've completed the task at hand. You are meticulous and thorough, unflappable in a crisis and hardworking to the end.

You approach your work with honesty and integrity, and your high standards in all areas of your life spill over into your career and ensure you accept nothing less than the best. You push for what you want and are not one for languishing in a job that isn't your number-one choice.

We all have to take the necessary steps to reach our chosen employment, but your impatience helps you gallop up the ladder.

When approaching a task, you get on with it with no fuss, no complaints. You hit the ground running and don't stop until you've reached the finish line. You take control and cling on to it tightly. You work best with other people who are clear and concise.

Your logical and analytical mind allows you to problem-solve with ease; you're clever and coolheaded, and this combination spurs you on to success. You command much respect at work, usually for all the right reasons – mixing as you do your calm and collected manner, with a steadfast work ethic, and decency and kindness for your fellow employees.

# Virgo:
## money and prosperity

Virgos are naturally high achievers and often go on to have great success in their working lives. Wise and analytical, you make practical decisions and are able to plan far ahead for your future. This partly stems from a nervous anxiety about what lies ahead and you tend to be a bit of a worrier when it comes to money matters.

A financial cushion is important to you in case the unexpected happens and you are keen to ensure you have the necessary security to keep yourself and your family afloat.

This means you're often very good at balancing your finances, knowing where every penny is heading and able to make rational choices when it comes to spending. Virgos tend to be wise when it comes to investing, often knowing how to play the game and where to go for the right advice.

Hard working by nature, you have your eyes on the prize as you squirrel away your earnings in order to save for a rainy day. You are also likely to be keen on investing in property if you possibly can, preferring to live in a shoebox that has your name on the deed, rather than rent somewhere more spacious.

# Virgo: health and well-being

Virgo's need for control over all aspects of their lives – and sometimes the lives of others – can be exhausting and when things don't go as planned, stress levels can seriously rocket. It's important to switch off and practice some self-care when needed – even when you don't think it is. Incorporating a regular yoga class into your schedule can work wonders for your anxiety levels, giving you the space to breathe. If you can fit it in, daily guided meditation for five or ten minutes will do you the world of good. It's important to look after your busy brain and ensure you don't burn out.

Regular outdoor exercise can also be a tonic for you and your creeping stress levels. Embrace outdoor pursuits that are good for the soul – get out in nature and go for a walk or a hike. You could even try some forest bathing – the Japanese have embraced this form of ecotherapy, which involves walking or immersing yourself in nature and consciously connecting with your surroundings. The benefits to your physical and mental health are manifold.

Wild or cold-water swimming is another way to use the benefits of nature to your advantage. Many fans of wild swimming claim to feel energized for the rest of the day following a dip, and the benefits of cold-water therapy are held in high esteem by many – look into the Wim Hof method if you want to know more.

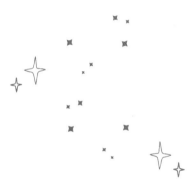

# *Part 3*

## YOUR HOROSCOPE AND YOU

This is where you start putting your knowledge into practice – it's time to build a birth chart. Over the following pages you'll learn how to do that and most importantly how to decode it. It might look complicated at first glance, but don't worry – all the elements and information you need to understand your chart are here in this chapter. We'll guide you through, step by step, and help you to make sense of it all. From your moon and rising signs, to the meanings hidden in the planets and houses, the mysteries of the night sky are about to be revealed.

# Using astrology for divination and guidance

By mapping out a birth chart and discovering the position of the planets and zodiac signs in the sky and which particular astrological house they were occupying when you were born, you can gain a deeper insight into yourself. Armed with this knowledge you can learn more about who you are, your motivations and what makes you tick. You could also gain a greater picture of who you might become, what prospects lie ahead and how you can potentially work them to your advantage.

Whether you feel misunderstood or simply want some clarity, you might find solace in the sky. When big decisions loom, you might look to astrology for comfort and reassurance. While astrology does not spell out the answers, it will give you much to ruminate on and relate to.

With the houses covering so many aspects of your life, and the planets and zodiac signs looking to your personality, there's a lot of coverage up there!

In the following pages you will learn how to cast your birth chart (this is much easier than it used to be, thanks to modern technology and the internet) and learn what all the segments and symbols mean; how to work out your moon and rising signs; and gain greater knowledge about the planets and houses, their influence on your life and how to interpret their meaning.

# *Dos and don'ts when interpreting the stars*

## DO

+ Remember astrology is all about guidance

+ Sleep on it before making any big decisions

+ Seek a reading from an experienced astrologer if you are worried or need clarity on your reading

## DON'T

+ Take things too literally – these are interpretations, presented for you to find meaning in them in relation to your life

+ Rush yourself – go at your own pace and all will become clear

+ Obsess over your results – tomorrow is another day and things could change

**A CHILD IS BORN
ON THAT DAY AND AT
THAT HOUR WHEN
THE CELESTIAL RAYS
ARE IN MATHEMATICAL
HARMONY WITH THEIR
INDIVIDUAL KARMA.**

SRI YUKTESWAR

# *How to create your own birth chart*

To create your birth chart you simply need to know the day on which you were born and the location. It is, however, vital that you know exactly what time you were born on that day. If you don't know, ask relatives, consult medical records or dig out your baby book – if you have one – because it is impossible to create an accurate birth chart without this information.

Sometimes referred to as a "natal chart", your birth chart is essentially a snapshot of the position of the planets and stars in the sky at the exact moment of your arrival on Earth. It's a wholly unique arrangement, never to be repeated, and can bring you so many valuable insights in your quest to better understand yourself.

Creating a birth chart used to be a painstaking process, but thanks to the power of the internet you can now be presented with yours in minutes. Try astro.com and opt for one of their free birth charts, from simple to complex; I say "simple" – even the simplest birth chart will look a bit indecipherable the first time you see one, but you'll soon get the hang of it.

TimePassages is a very user-friendly paid-for app where you can create a birth chart and read daily horoscopes based on your personal information and astrological transits – as well as compare your chart with a friend or partner's – should you want to delve a little deeper.

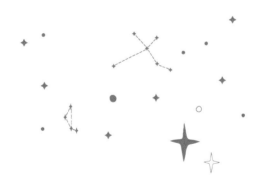

# An example birth chart

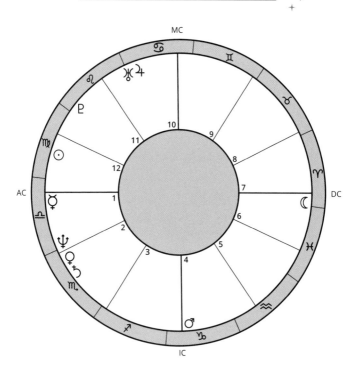

# *Symbols*

| ARIES | TAURUS | GEMINI | CANCER |

| LEO | VIRGO | LIBRA | SCORPIO |

| SAGITTARIUS | CAPRICORN | AQUARIUS | PISCES |

## PLANET SYMBOLS

| SUN | MOON |

| MERCURY | VENUS | MARS | JUPITER | SATURN |

| URANUS | NEPTUNE | PLUTO |

# How to decipher your birth chart

It's a good idea to keep an open mind when reviewing your birth chart. Be flexible, be imaginative and be prepared to take on the challenges it presents. Explore the potential it offers and be open to suggestions you might not previously have expected.

We've talked about the signs of the zodiac already, and in the following pages we'll look at the planets and the houses. These are the most important elements of the birth chart.

You will find around the outer wheel the 12 signs of the zodiac, while the inner 12 segments that overlap these are the houses.

The line across the middle is the horizon, with "AC" for ascendant, or rising sign, and "DC" for descendant. Look to the vertical line and "MC" is for midheaven and "IC" for *imum coeli* (loosely translating as "bottom of the sky").

Now it's time to work out what it all means. Follow the instructions on the following pages to find out how.

## THE PLANETS

Look at the planets one by one and where they are placed on the chart. The simplest way to explain these is that the planets tell you "what", the sign it is transitioning through tells you "how" and "why", and the house the planet appears in represents the area of life to which this is relevant. As the sixth sign of the zodiac, Virgo rules the sixth house. This means that this particular house is associated with Virgo energy. Looking at the example birth chart on page 70, the Moon is transitioning through Aries and Pisces and the sixth house. From this we can take the Moon to signify hospitality, Aries to stand for productivity and Pisces to represent structure – perhaps finding the perfect home is very important to you – in the sixth house, which symbolizes health and well-being.

## PLANET CLUSTERS

Clusters of planets on the chart can also be revealing. The upper hemisphere of the chart represents your public life, while the lower hemisphere represents your private life. The west half represents freedom, while the east side represents fate. If there are more planets on one side than the other then this sways your reading.

## LUNAR NODES

The lunar nodes are represented by the symbol ☊. These are the points at which the moon intercepts the sphere. Each astrology chart has a north and a south node, with the south node positioned directly opposite the north. Because the south node represents your past, who you have been, your instinctive behavior and your comfort zone, it doesn't tend to feature on birth charts, but is instead reserved for astrological readings later in life; the north node represents the opposite to the south node – where you should be heading in life, your aspirations and how you should challenge yourself to grow. The zodiac signs these two nodes fall into represent what these past and future characteristics should look like.

For example, on the birth chart on page 70, the north node falls into Capricorn, suggesting your future lies in finding the perfect career, rising to the top and being bold when making big decisions.

**THE STARRY VAULT
OF HEAVEN IS IN TRUTH
THE OPEN BOOK OF
COSMIC PROJECTION.**

CARL JUNG

## How to discover your moon sign

Your moon sign refers to the astrological sign the Moon was travelling through at the time of your birth. The Moon takes two-and-a-half days to travel through each sign, so around one month to complete a cycle of all the signs of the zodiac.

Understanding your moon sign is important because it speaks of your emotional nature – your fears, longings, obsessions and everything in between. It is often called the "soul of your identity" – the subconscious part of you that remains hidden and perhaps you don't even know that well. Learning more about your moon sign can help to unlock these hidden traits and help you to understand yourself better.

Some call your moon sign your "inner child", your closely guarded emotional centre. It can have a big impact on your mood and the way your emotions make their way to the surface.

You will know your sun sign, but it's important to calculate your moon sign too in order to gain the bigger picture. You will feel incomplete without it.

## How to calculate
## your moon sign

In the past, in order to determine your moon sign, you would have had to look up your time and date of birth in a planetary ephemeris - an extensive compendium of tables charting the Moon's position throughout the days, months and years. You can find your moon sign on your birth chart. For example, on the birth chart on page 70, the moon sign falls into Pisces, suggesting that you can sometimes let your emotions overwhelm you.

You do not need to create your birth chart to find out your moon sign, however. If you're after a quick answer you can use an online calculator such as lunarium.co.uk/calculators/moonsign. You will need to know the exact time of your birth, as a few minutes either way could push you to a different sign entirely.

# *Understanding your moon sign*

**Aries –** You are an impatient soul, powering through life at a stressful pace. It can be hard to plan ahead when all you think about is what is happening right now.

**Taurus –** You take things slowly and cautiously, remaining calm and paying attention to every detail. You are tactile and feel the need to keep people close.

**Gemini –** You thrive on learning and taking in new information – whether through interactions with others or reading books.

**Cancer –** Security is very important to you and there is a deep-rooted urge to also keep those around you safe.

**Leo –** You love being showered with praise and seek it wherever you can. You are keen to nurture your own talents and help others find theirs too.

**Virgo –** You are practical when it comes to taking care of yourself and others. Well-being is important to you and self-care high up on your priorities.

**Libra –** You love company and are drawn to people with whom you can create easy friendships. Well-being is high up on your agenda, particularly when it involves calm and peace.

**Scorpio –** You wear your emotions on your sleeve and can find it hard to hold back. Try a fast-paced workout if you need to shake off these feelings.

**Sagittarius –** You like your own space and the freedom to do things your way. You prefer to travel solo and deal with your emotions on your own.

**Capricorn –** You are a fan of routine – structure works for you and helps you to navigate day-to-day life as well as retain a feeling of control.

**Aquarius –** You don't follow the crowd and always want to explore alternative options. A sense of community is important to you as you seek like-minded folk.

**Pisces –** Your emotions can often confuse you – as can how to deal with those of other people. Often a little time out is the ideal solution.

# *What is a rising sign?*

Your rising sign, also known as your "ascendant", is the constellation that was rising on the eastern horizon at the time of your birth – and it's just as important as your sun sign!

As with your sun sign, there are 12 rising signs – from Aries to Pisces. While your sun sign reflects your personality, your rising sign reflects how you act.

For example, looking at the birth chart on page 70, if your sun sign is Virgo you might have an industrious and practical outlook, but with rising sign Libra you might act in an utterly charming way. (See pages 18–23 for an overview of the zodiac signs and traits.)

Your rising sign is associated with the first house of your chart (see page 85 for more about the houses), so it's all about new beginnings and self-identity. Your sun sign represents a bigger picture of you, while your rising sign represents the surface of your personality, a first impression if you will.

## How to calculate your rising sign

These days we only need to search online to discover our rising sign, but in the past astrologers had to put pen to paper to work it out.

Your rising sign is very specific to the time of day you were born and is essential for an accurate birth chart. The rising sign changes frequently, so this information is key. If you've ever encountered a pushy astrologer who insisted you give up this information – this is why! With all 12 signs of the Zodiac rising in a 24-hour period, each takes a 2-hour window, which can then be connected to the time of your birth. If you are born at sunrise, your sun and rising signs will be the same.

Twins born 15 minutes apart could well have different rising signs, meaning their birth charts – and therefore their personalities – could differ greatly from each other.

While you can gather all of this information from your birth chart, if you are after a swift answer you can calculate your rising sign here: astrosofa.com/ascendant.

# *How to calculate your descendant*

Your descendant is the sign that was setting on the western horizon at the time of your birth, it lies directly opposite your ascendant, in the seventh house, which represents relationships (see page 85 for more about the houses).

The descendant describes your desires, who you get along with and who you are attracted to.

It represents external obstacles that challenge you on a daily basis and what you desire but cannot reach.

Your descendant sign is important in understanding your behavior in relationships and reflects experiences that can help you to understand issues in a partnership. For example, in the birth chart on page 70, the descendant is Aries, suggesting you are patient and polite, are attracted to risk-takers, but need to find balance in relationships.

To discover your descendant, look at your birth chart or use the same link you used to calculate your ascendant and scroll down for your full astrological profile: astrosofa.com/ascendant.

# Understanding the planets in your birth chart

With each planet reflecting a part of our psyche, there is much to be gained from a deeper understanding of their meaning. The planets indicate how we react to people and situations, and outline our dreams and desires. Don't worry if some of the houses on your birth chart do not contain any planets – this is quite common! Each planet has a sign that it naturally rules – a sign that it is often found frequenting. Use the information below when interpreting your birth chart and refer to page 17 for your sun-sign-specific guidance on the planets.

**The Sun** is our ego, will and determination, orbiting all the signs of the zodiac in the space of a calendar year.

**The Moon** reflects the part of ourselves that remains hidden, our memories and inner emotions. It transitions into a new sign every two-and-a-half days.

**Mercury** is the planet of communication, news and travel. It can also reflect gossip and rumor.

**Venus** is the planet of love, romance, sensuality and beauty. It helps us understand our love for others, but also things.

**Mars** is the planet of energy, action and conflict.

**Saturn** is the planet of commitment and stability. It also represents the restrictions placed on us.

**Jupiter** stands for spiritual growth and helps us to understand any emotional issues we may have.

**Neptune** is often referred to as "poetry of the soul", reflecting our deep-rooted emotions and creativity.

**Uranus** represents rebellion and the fight for injustice – in both our personal lives and on a global scale.

**Pluto** looks to change and how it can allow us to grow and achieve our dreams. This is the planet that forces us to face our fears and conquer them.

# Understanding the houses in your birth chart

While your birth chart is divided into 12 sections that represent the sun signs of the zodiac, there are another 12 sections overlapping these called the "houses". Each house represents a different aspect of your everyday life, from your career, to travel, to love and more. Every planet on your chart is located in both a sun sign and a house, and their positions are key to deciphering your birth chart and understanding more about your inner workings. The houses are complex and far-reaching; the pages that follow offer a brief insight to get you started, but if you want to probe deeper refer to Resources on page 125 to find out even more.

## FIRST HOUSE: PERSONALITY

This is the house of the self; it represents you, the body you were born with and your temperament. This is the house that symbolizes birth and new beginnings, reflecting how we view our life, and how our earliest encounters have impacted us and shaped our world. When planets move into this house, our goals are manifested and fresh new ideas begin to form.

**Planets in this house**

Sun – Self-development
Moon – Deep feelings
Mercury – Connection
Venus – Beauty
Mars – Strength
Jupiter – Optimism
Saturn – Foresight
Uranus – Individuality
Neptune – Glamour
Pluto – Control

**Zodiac signs in this house**

Aries – Motivation
Taurus – Balance
Gemini – Communication
Cancer – Protection
Leo – Action
Virgo – Order
Libra – Grace
Scorpio – Self-defense
Sagittarius – Vision
Capricorn – Planning
Aquarius – Clarity
Pisces – Imagination

## SECOND HOUSE: POSSESSIONS AND MONEY

This house is all about material possessions and personal finances. It tells you about your attitude towards money – do you love it or hate it? It also gives you an insight into your personal finances – perhaps they are a source of concern, perhaps you're good at saving for a rainy day, or you could be rather frivolous – and how you earn it and spend it. Beyond finances, anything to do with worth and value can be found in this house – what we consider valuable in life and how we value ourselves.

**Planets in this house**

Sun – Independence
Moon – Security
Mercury – Communication
Venus – Sensuality
Mars – Ambition
Jupiter – Confidence
Saturn – Frugality
Uranus – Change
Neptune – Charity
Pluto – Survival

**Zodiac signs in this house**

Aries – Self-motivation
Taurus – Accumulation
Gemini – Light-heartedness
Cancer – Possessiveness
Leo – Pride
Virgo – Thriftiness
Libra – Equality
Scorpio – Privacy
Sagittarius – Frivolity
Capricorn – Planning
Aquarius – Sharing
Pisces – Generosity

## THIRD HOUSE: COMMUNICATION

This house is all about how you communicate with those around you. How you express yourself and build relationships with others in your life – whether friends, family, co-workers, neighbors or those in the wider community – is at play here and when planets move into this house you can receive information about your network of associations. This house also has a strong focus on the language element of communication and also the relationships you have with your siblings.

**Planets in this house**

Sun – Language
Moon – Education
Mercury – Connection
Venus – Harmony
Mars – Competition
Jupiter – Optimism
Saturn – Authority
Uranus – Single-
    mindedness
Neptune – Intuition
Pluto – Learning

**Zodiac signs in this house**

Aries – Rivalry
Taurus – Learning
Gemini – Connection
Cancer – Protection
Leo – Confidence
Virgo – Organization
Libra – Equality
Scorpio – Education
Sagittarius – Adventure
Capricorn – Planning
Aquarius – Rationality
Pisces – Imagination

## FOURTH HOUSE: HOME AND FAMILY

This house reflects your home, the place you regard as your safe haven or where your family resides. It's about where you feel a sense of belonging, sanctuary and security. The family in this house refers not just to your relations, but the family you choose for yourself through friends, neighbors and those in your local community. This house reflects your relationship with the maternal figure(s) in your life and looks to the situations in which you feel loved and looked after.

| Planets in this house | Zodiac signs in this house |
|---|---|
| Sun – Identity | Aries – Rivalry |
| Moon – Privacy | Taurus – Security |
| Mercury – Conversation | Gemini – Loyalty |
| Venus – Peace | Cancer – Protection |
| Mars – Conflict | Leo – Pride |
| Jupiter – Travel | Virgo – Duty |
| Saturn – Stability | Libra – Diplomacy |
| Uranus – Independence | Scorpio – Privacy |
| Neptune – Sanctuary | Sagittarius – Welcome |
| Pluto – Renovation | Capricorn – Organization |
| | Aquarius – Community |
| | Pisces – Music |

# FIFTH HOUSE: CREATIVITY AND PLEASURE

As well as creativity and pleasure, this house is also linked with leisure, romance and those tiny bringers of joy, children, as well as our legacy. This house is all about what makes you feel good and brings you joy – whether that's getting your teeth into a creative project, feeling the rush of a confidence boost thanks to a compliment or career success, or the excitement of a new partner or life milestone. Risk-taking also falls into this house, so gamblers and extreme-sports enthusiasts take note.

**Planets in this house**

Sun – Attention
Moon – Playfulness
Mercury – Impulsivity
Venus – Communication
Mars – Competition
Jupiter – Fertility
Saturn – Strategy
Uranus – Originality
Neptune – Artistry
Pluto – Transformation

**Zodiac signs in this house**

Aries – Action
Taurus – Grounding
Gemini – Romantic connection
Cancer – Caretaking
Leo – Joyfulness
Virgo – Humility
Libra – Perfection
Scorpio – Loyalty
Sagittarius – Travel
Capricorn – Caution
Aquarius – Value
Pisces – Romance

## SIXTH HOUSE: HEALTH AND WELL-BEING

As well as health and well-being, this house reflects your daily routines, which include jobs around the house and perhaps the more mundane tasks that you don't tend to give a second thought. Here is where to look for help in streamlining your schedules.

While the body you are born with is reflected in the first house, it is in this house that the focus lands on the body you have created over the course of your lifetime. Self-care, work–life balance, as well as mental and physical health are all covered here.

**Planets in this house**

Sun – Purpose
Moon – Hospitality
Mercury – Networking
Venus – Unity
Mars – Movement
Jupiter – Satisfaction
Saturn – Construction
Uranus – Change
Neptune – Music
Pluto – Nutrition

**Zodiac signs in this house**

Aries – Productivity
Taurus – Calm
Gemini – Dexterity
Cancer – Caretaking
Leo – Authority
Virgo – Detail
Libra – Diplomacy
Scorpio – Activity
Sagittarius – Freedom
Capricorn – Attention
Aquarius – Equality
Pisces – Structure

## SEVENTH HOUSE: RELATIONSHIPS

Directly across from the first house, the seventh house reflects your life-changing relationships – not just romantic partners, but all significant relationships in your life. This house will look at negative as well as positive aspects of those relationships – offering potential insight into any disagreements you might have experienced among your nearest and dearest.

**Planets in this house**
Sun – Individuality
Moon – Sensitivity
Mercury – Knowledge
Venus – Value
Mars – Assertiveness
Jupiter – Motivation
Saturn – Commitment
Uranus – Independence
Neptune – Longing
Pluto – Transformation

**Zodiac signs in this house**
Aries – Equality
Taurus – Stability
Gemini – Variety
Cancer – Sentimentality
Leo – Desire
Virgo – Grounding
Libra – Compromise
Scorpio – Intensity
Sagittarius – Company
Capricorn – Security
Aquarius – Supportiveness
Pisces – Selflessness

# EIGHTH HOUSE: SEX, DEATH AND TRANSFORMATION

This is the house in which we experience the darker aspects of life – emotional crises, loss and devastation – as well as the rituals, trials and tribulations of our existence. This house also reflects our intense romantic partnerships and adaptability to the ever-changing nature of our lives. This house teaches us that we need to embrace compromise in order to move forward, accept change and learn to derive power and inner strength from loss.

**Planets in this house**

Sun – Exploration
Moon – Intuition
Mercury – Secrecy
Venus – Diplomacy
Mars – Decisiveness
Jupiter – Positivity
Saturn – Boundaries
Uranus – Clarity
Neptune – Connection
Pluto – Power

**Zodiac signs in this house**

Aries – Impulsivity
Taurus – Investment
Gemini – Exploration
Cancer – Privacy
Leo – Financial success
Virgo – Catastrophe
Libra – Equality
Scorpio – Lust
Sagittarius – Risk-taking
Capricorn – Independence
Aquarius – Rationality
Pisces – Excitement

## NINTH HOUSE: PHILOSOPHY AND ADVENTURE

This house looks ahead towards what we don't yet know – what lies beyond the horizon. Travel and higher education are also represented here – and those with birth charts showing planets in their ninth house are often extremely inquisitive and adventurous when it comes to travel. This house represents uncharted territory and curiosity – searching for a greater understanding of ourselves – as well as faith and politics.

**Planets in this house**
Sun – Confidence
Moon – Wanderlust
Mercury – Language
Venus – Creativity
Mars – Fearlessness
Jupiter – Teaching
Saturn – Caution
Uranus – Enlightenment
Neptune – Spirituality
Pluto – Education

**Zodiac signs in this house**
Aries – Independence
Taurus – Patience
Gemini – Curiosity
Cancer – Connection
Leo – Luxury
Virgo – Preparedness
Libra – Equality
Scorpio – Education
Sagittarius – Limitless
Capricorn – Ambition
Aquarius – Community
Pisces – Escape

## TENTH HOUSE: CAREER

As well as your professional aspirations, this house also takes in social status and popularity. If you have planets in the tenth house on your birth chart you are no doubt an ambitious person when it comes to work life – and you know how to socialize with gusto. If you are feeling somewhat in limbo, this house may help to guide you towards your calling. Career changes are afoot when planets transition into this house.

**Planets in this house**

Sun – Identity
Moon – Caring
Mercury – Networking
Venus – Diplomacy
Mars – Competition
Jupiter – Possibility
Saturn – Responsibility
Uranus – Independence
Neptune – Creativity
Pluto – Influence

**Zodiac signs in this house**

Aries – Self-starter
Taurus – Loyalty
Gemini – Variety
Cancer – Nurturing
Leo – Self-promotion
Virgo – Creativity
Libra – Diplomacy
Scorpio – Determination
Sagittarius – Achievement
Capricorn – Organization
Aquarius – Teamwork
Pisces – Compassion

## ELEVENTH HOUSE: FRIENDSHIP

This is the house that recognizes our social circle, and is where we find our place in the networks and groups in our lives. Here we find friendship, teamwork and common goals represented, as well as our support network, acquaintances and the way in which we spend time with those in our lives. Our social and political values come to the fore in this house, as does our ability to work with others to improve situations.

**Planets in this house**

Sun – Community
Moon – Extroversion
Mercury – Networking
Venus – Charm
Mars – Competition
Jupiter – Broadmindedness
Saturn – Commitment
Uranus – Freedom
Neptune – Self-sacrifice
Pluto – Empowerment

**Zodiac signs in this house**

Aries – Energy
Taurus – Constancy
Gemini – Diversity
Cancer – Safety
Leo – Leadership
Virgo – Caring
Libra – Harmony
Scorpio – Force
Sagittarius – Initiative
Capricorn – Control
Aquarius – Equality
Pisces – Sympathy

## TWELFTH HOUSE: SACRIFICE

Sometimes known as the house of the unconscious, the twelfth house is also referred to as "the darkness before the dawn" – sitting just below the horizon, finishing off the houses before the cycle begins again. The "unconscious" speaks of all things without physical form, such as dreams, emotions and secrets. Planets take on an otherworldly quality in this house and this is where your good deeds are recognized.

| **Planets in this house** | **Zodiac signs in this house** |
|---|---|
| Sun – Purpose | Aries – Initiative |
| Moon – Compassion | Taurus – Relaxation |
| Mercury – Imagination | Gemini – Ambition |
| Venus – Self-reflection | Cancer – Caring |
| Mars – Courage | Leo – Creativity |
| Jupiter – Generosity | Virgo – Thoughtfulness |
| Saturn – Dedication | Libra – Balance |
| Uranus – Freedom | Scorpio – Intuition |
| Neptune – Charity | Sagittarius – Escape |
| Pluto – Acceptance | Capricorn – Structure |
| | Aquarius – Recharge |
| | Pisces – Boundaries |

# Part 4

## ASTROLOGY FOR SELF-CARE

We all need a little self-care in our lives and astrology can help steer you towards practices most suited to your sun sign and characteristics. As a Virgo, you are constantly analyzing your life and surroundings, overthinking every situation and work event. Prone to nervous thought, sometimes this can mean you lie awake at the end of a long day, your brain filled with noise and chatter. Your urges to control every aspect of your life can leave you feeling tense, so it's important to incorporate some deep relaxation into your self-care routine. Many Virgos find relaxing and mindful activities, such as yoga and meditation, keep the mind and body happy, while others look to channel their creativity into journaling to relieve any tension What helps you to de-stress? The following pages offer some ideas to help you find the methods best suited to you.

# *How to use astrology to guide self-care practices*

By aligning your self-care practices with your sun sign, you can really boost their healing power. It's worth doing the research to get the most out of your downtime and rest. When it comes to yoga there are poses that offer a greater benefit to one sign over another, according to your personality and behaviors; and you will find favor in the crystals that match your sun sign, allowing energy to flow more freely with those assigned to you.

The following pages contain self-care rituals and practices specific to you and your sign. From tarot to crystals, the celestial body and your chakras, and de-stressing techniques, as well as the types of exercise that could suit you best.

As a Virgo, it's important to let go of control every once in a while, and allow your thoughts time to pause. Make room for some self-care in your life and take some time out to relax and improve your sleep. You could try writing your thoughts and wishes in a journal or incorporating five to ten minutes of guided meditation into your day to banish any unhelpful thoughts.

# *Dos and don'ts*

## DO

+ Go at your own pace; self-care is not a race

+ What feels right; not every suggestion will be the one for you

+ Allow the guidance to help you to change bad habits

## DON'T

+ Push yourself too hard; if you have a minor injury but the guidance is to do some strenuous exercise, give it a miss until you're feeling better

+ Give up things you love just because they're not mentioned as specific to your sign

+ Take risks if something doesn't feel right – stay safe and comfortable

**WE ARE MERELY THE
STARS' TENNIS-BALLS,
STRUCK AND BANDIED
WHICH WAY PLEASE THEM.**

JOHN WEBSTER

# *Rituals to help Virgo de-stress and unwind*

While Virgos love to socialize and could talk all night, it's important to embrace stillness and quiet to truly de-stress. If you have trouble sleeping as unhelpful thoughts bat around your head, you'll find that making room for quiet time helps to improve this situation and hopefully affords you the deep sleep you need to function properly.

A busy brain can be hard to quieten when there's been a lot going on during the day, so try heading to bed early for some restorative sleep and introduce a bedtime routine to really wind down. Spray lavender on your pillow and around your bedroom, banish screens for at least an hour before bed and get comfortable with a good book or magazine. If you need some help dropping off, investigate Calm, an app designed to help you de-stress and alleviate anxiety through guided meditation, sleep stories and soothing sounds. You'll likely find you don't reach the end of a sleep story as you are lulled into a deep slumber. Try the free version to see if it works for you before you sign up.

Positive affirmations will also help you to feel better about yourself. A good morning – or any time – ritual for you might be to practice some affirmations either in the mirror or in a quiet space by yourself. Affirmations are very personal to the individual, but if you need some guidance or a jumping-off point, start with something simple like "I am strong", "I am capable", "I can do this!", before trying something more specific.

# *Yoga poses for Virgo*

The benefits of yoga are far-reaching, from increasing flexibility, improving muscle strength and tone, boosting energy, promoting circulation and restorative sleep, to bringing you a sense of zen and relaxation. The following yoga poses are ideal for you – and if you want to explore further, try Kundalini or Iyengar styles of yoga for more exploratory forms of the practice.

Always make sure you warm up first and don't push your body. If you haven't tried yoga before, consider joining a class taught by an experienced yoga practitioner.

## TREE POSE

Stand with your feet together, shift your weight to one foot and spread out your toes. Slowly lift your other foot and place it on your inner thigh or on your calf – be careful not to press it to your knee. Bring your palms together in the center of your chest. If you wobble, focus on something – a spot on the floor perhaps – to help you keep your balance.

To take this pose further take your prayer hands and stretch them up above your head. Lift your chin and enjoy this stretch for several breaths. Then swap to the other side and perform the stretch again.

## CHILD'S POSE

This simple and calming pose can be done at any time. If you find yourself restless in the middle of the night, try doing this pose on your bed to relax your body and get ready to sleep again. Kneel with your knees hip-width apart and your toes touching each other. Exhale and fold yourself forward, resting your torso between your thighs. Tuck your chin under and stretch your arms out on the mat in front of you. Let the weight of your shoulders open the shoulder blades and breathe. Rest here for 30 seconds to a few minutes, whatever feels natural and needed.

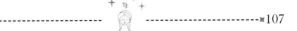

## TRIANGLE POSE

This lengthening and strengthening pose is good for the thighs, torso, hips, groin, hamstrings, calves, shoulders and spine.

Stand on your mat with your feet together, shoulders back and your arms at your sides (this is known as mountain pose). Move your feet so they are about a yard apart. Stretch your arms out either side with palms down, parallel to the floor. Turn your right foot out by 90 degrees and your left foot in slightly. Turn your head to look over your right arm, to your fingertips. Strengthen your left leg and root your heel into the floor. Hinge at your hips to bring your right arm down to your ankle, if you can reach, and stretch your left arm upwards, fingertips reaching for the sky. Hold this pose for a few breaths before swapping to the other side.

## SEATED SPINAL POSE

This stretches the chest, shoulders and back, and opens up the hips – great to relieve neck and shoulder pain after a long day at work or to remove any unwanted tension built up over a day of rushing about.

Sit cross-legged with your back straight. Place your left hand on your right knee and the fingertips of your right hand on the mat behind you. Inhale to sit up as tall as you can and lengthen your spine; exhale and twist to the right. Hold this pose for a few breaths before switching to the other side.

# THERE IS NO BETTER BOAT THAN A HOROSCOPE TO HELP A MAN CROSS OVER THE SEA OF LIFE.

VARAHA MIHIRA

# *Exercise for Virgo*

Virgos are ambitious and competitive, which makes you a driven team player. It's likely you take part in a sport regularly – perhaps once a week – that involves both playing and socializing with others, and you might even be captain or involved in the organization in some way.

If you're a runner, you prefer to head out with others and running clubs are a good option. Your competitiveness doesn't rest here, however, and it's likely you're always pushing yourself to run that bit further, that bit quicker. The uber-competitive among you might even be eyeing up an ultra-marathon as something to tick off your bucket list – certainly not for the faint-hearted!

Pilates will also serve you well to build core strength and outdoor workouts can be a good option to give your brain a boost in a green space where you can fill your lungs with fresh air.

Is there any outdoor fitness equipment available near where you live? If not, why not improvise to keep yourself outdoors and immersed in nature. Many exercises from press-ups and squats, to burpees and jumping jacks can be performed pretty much anywhere.

Body-conditioning martial arts could also be beneficial to relieve stress. Try Taekwondo to build strength, stamina and patience. Using concise punching and kicking techniques alongside mental strength training; this ancient martial art's history is rooted in self-defense, with mind and body participating in equal measure.

# *Crystals*

Naturally occurring crystals contain piezoelectric and pyroelectric properties that cause them to vibrate. This, along with the fact that they are also conductors of heat and electricity, has led many to believe that they have the ability to transform your energy levels, help you find love and restore your health.

Crystals have been used in healing for thousands of years and evidence of this can be found in ancient texts. The vibrations are thought to help restore the body's natural healing mechanisms, as well as encouraging a sense of balance, calm and well-being. This type of practice is called "vibrational medicine".

People often select crystals according to their color as well as their properties, and their sun sign and birth date can come into play here too. Choosing crystals with your sun sign in mind can help to align you for a more successful experience. Bearing in mind the celestial body (see page 36) and matching crystals to the chakra related to your sun sign (see page 122) will also bring the most benefits.

| Chakra | Location | Color | Emotional and physical associations |
|--------|----------|-------|-------------------------------------|
| Root | Base of spine | Red | Feeling grounded, independent |
| Sacral | Just below navel | Orange | Acceptance, well-being, pleasure |
| Solar plexus | Base of ribcage | Yellow | Confidence, self-control, self-esteem |
| Heart | Centre of chest | Green | Love, joy, inner peace |
| Throat | Base of throat | Blue | Communication, self-expression |
| Third eye | Above and between brows | Indigo | Intuition, decision-making |
| Crown | Top of head | Violet | A feeling of connection, spirituality |

## CRYSTALS ACCORDING TO ZODIAC SIGN

**Aries** – Red jasper, carnelian, citrine

**Taurus** – Smoky quartz, amazonite, selenite

**Gemini** – Shungite, amazonite, tiger's eye

**Cancer** – Selenite, labradorite, red jasper

**Leo** – Tiger's eye, rose quartz, garnet

**Virgo** – Amazonite, amethyst, fluorite

**Libra** – Tiger's eye, amethyst, bloodstone

**Scorpio** – Pink tourmaline, amethyst, raindrop azurite

**Sagittarius** – Lepidolite, smoky quartz, shungite

**Capricorn** – Rose quartz, garnet, smoky quartz

**Aquarius** – Lepidolite, amethyst, tourmalinated quartz

**Pisces** – Clear quartz, carnelian, chrysocolla

## CLEANSE YOUR CRYSTALS

Preparing your crystals before use is important in order to remove any negative or old energy. Rinse them under running water for a minute and leave to dry outside in the fresh air. Then submerge your crystals in salt water and leave out to air dry. Finally, leave your crystals to bathe in moonlight or sunlight for 12 hours. Now they are ready to use.

## SELF-CARE WITH CRYSTALS

You might want to try using crystals to create a calming space in your home, or an area in which you want to nurture creativity. Follow these simple steps to shift energy and transform your safe space.

✦ **Choose a quiet space in your home – perhaps an area of your living room or bedroom. Make sure this is a place where you can have a few moments away from any noise or other people, it is comfortable and you will be able to relax.**

✦ **Allow air to flow through the space in order to rid it of any "dead energy". Then do some more physical dusting and clean it up, clearing away any dust or cobwebs, and decluttering so only a few things remain.**

✦ **Add some crystals to bring a calm energy to the space – quartz and amethyst work well for this, promoting healing, cleansing and harmony.**

✦ **Put the crystals in a place where they will catch the natural light, and make sure they each have some space and are not touching each other.**

# Tarot

Tarot can be used for divination and anyone can do a reading – you don't need to visit a psychic or be one yourself to dabble with the deck. Either perform your reading yourself or ask a friend to do it and take it in turns. Tarot can offer insight and guidance by asking a question and interpreting cards pulled at random from the deck. Each of the 78 cards holds a unique meaning in relation to the question being asked.

The cards are made up of the major and minor arcana. The 22 major arcana cards feature some you might have heard of before, such as the Sun, the Moon, the Fool, Death and the Lovers. These represent karmic influences and themes in your life. If one of these appears in your reading, it often signifies the need to reflect on its life lessons. Each zodiac sign is ruled by a card from the major arcana. In the case of Virgo, the card is the Hermit – a figure that encourages you to find comfort in solitude and use time by yourself to think constructively about your life.

The minor arcana features 56 cards grouped into four suits of 14 each; ten of these are numbered, along with a Page, Knight, Queen and King. These cards represent situations, guide you to make choices and reflect your state of mind.

Tarot itself is interpreted in different ways, with some believing the answers come from spirits or angels, while others favoring the explanation of synchronicity where the cards drawn are meaningfully related. If this is something that interests you, you're best to research tarot in more detail to understand the meanings behind each card, but the following pages will get you started with a few tips on how to set yourself up. With a little guidance, you can unlock the symbolism and begin a journey of self-discovery.

## CHOOSING A DECK

It is supposedly bad luck to buy your first tarot deck yourself and believed that it should be given as a gift. However, this is often disregarded as archaic superstition, so if you're not bothered by that then go ahead and buy a deck yourself! It's important you have a good relationship with the deck of cards you end up using, so make sure you like the illustrations they feature. There are hundreds of different decks available, so do some research and choose some you like the look of. If you feel lost amid the variety, go for the ever-popular Rider-Waite-Smith deck.

## ENERGIZING AND CLEANSING YOUR CARDS

A new deck needs to be energized, so once you've taken your cards out of their shiny wrapping be sure to give them a thorough shuffle. The best way to do this is to fan out the cards on a table and swirl them around until you're satisfied they're well and truly mixed up. Don't be precious, you want some of the cards to be upside down in order to give reversals in your readings, so swirl, mix and swirl again.

When you haven't used your deck for a while, it's a good idea to give it a cleanse to banish any negative energy. There are several ways you can do this: shuffle the deck and knock on it three times; place the cards on a window ledge overnight where they will be bathed in moonlight; burn some dried sage and pass the deck though the smoke a few times.

## SETTING THE SCENE

In the beginning, it's a good idea to choose a space to practice where you will have some peace and quiet, and can give the deck your full attention. Choose a space that is calm and uncluttered – you want it to have a positive energy, so you could select a few items to help create the perfect space.

## SETTING YOUR INTENTION

During a reading, it's vital you keep the positive energy flowing around you. An easy way to do this is to bathe the room in bright, white light – this will banish negative energy and keep it at bay for the duration of your reading.

## READING AND QUESTIONING

Beginners are best off starting with a three-card spread, such as past, present and future. Make sure you have your question in your mind as you shuffle the deck. Cards that fly out of the deck while shuffling are symbolic. Deal three cards, face up, in front of you – past, present and future.

The more detailed the question you ask, the more detail you will have returned in your answer. Try to avoid vague questions or those that could have a simple "yes" or "no" answer. Think of questions that are more likely to open up a conversation. As a Virgo, you might want to ask detailed questions related to your future and what your finances might look like. Will you ever buy the house of your dreams? Where might you end up? Ask the cards how it will all pan out.

WE NEED NOT FEEL
ASHAMED OF FLIRTING
WITH THE ZODIAC. THE
ZODIAC IS WELL WORTH
FLIRTING WITH.

D. H. LAWRENCE

# *Chakras*

If you're into yoga, you might be familiar with chakras, or you might like to learn more. Rooted in Hinduism but practiced by many outside the faith, chakras are considered to be life forces that circulate energy to certain parts of our body. When the stresses and strains of life cause these to become blocked, we can feel the impact and it helps to work to unblock them. The best way to do this is by promoting the flow of energy via meditation, chakra-specific yoga poses and breathing exercises.

There are seven main chakras – the root, sacral, solar plexus, heart, throat, third eye and crown – these are separate from the parts of the body associated with each sun sign and instead correspond to a person's characteristics.

## SUN SIGNS AND CHAKRAS

**Aries** – solar plexus, located in the abdomen, a source of self-belief and power

**Taurus** – heart chakra, the energy of which brings empathic skills

**Gemini** – throat chakra, associated with communication and creativity

**Cancer** – third eye chakra, located on the forehead and believed to be the centre of the soul

**Leo** – crown chakra, representing thinking, understanding and arriving at solutions easily

**Virgo** – throat chakra, signifying clear communication and public speaking

**Libra** – heart chakra, the source of emotional healing and building bonds with others

**Scorpio** – solar plexus chakra, which helps to battle fears and control emotions

**Sagittarius** – sacral chakra, bringing optimism and passion

**Capricorn** – root chakra, located at the base of the spine, promoting good mental and physical health

**Aquarius** – root chakra, helping to stay grounded and supportive

**Pisces** – sacral chakra, promoting sensuality, emotion and creativity

## *Farewell*

How are you feeling about the zodiac now? You've learned so much! It's likely you've had a few "aha" moments while reading this book, with familiar scenarios and characteristics floating off the page. Many of us long to be understood better and astrology can provide some comfort amid the complexities of modern life.

Hopefully you now feel armed with the knowledge and insight you need to embark on the next phase of your journey. It's time for you to draw your own conclusions about who you are and why you behave the way you do – and the stars can help. The mystery of the zodiac is vast, but it is there to be unraveled and if you're up for the challenge you will certainly reap the rewards.

# Resources

## BOOKS

Goodman, Linda *Sun Signs* (1999, Pan)

Parker, Derek and Parker, Julia *Parkers' Astrology* (2021, Dorling Kindersley)

Taylor, Carole *Using the Wisdom of the Stars in Your Everyday Life* (2018, Dorling Kindersley)

## WEBSITES AND APPS

Astro.com – a vast free resource for beginners and experienced astrologers; start by drawing up your birth chart using this website and move on from there

Linda-goodman.com – a useful forum dedicated to the late astrologer, where people share their astrological experience

TimePassages – user-friendly paid-for astrology app where you can create a birth chart as well as read daily horoscopes and compare your chart with a friend or partner's

Co-Star – popular astrology app (basic version is free) with slick design; a useful tool with real-time readings gleaned from NASA data and a wealth of information and insight

**ASTROLOGY IS LIKE
A GAME OF CHESS WITH
AN INVISIBLE PARTNER.**

NOEL TYL

# Check out the rest of the series...

THE ZODIAC GUIDE TO
ARIES

THE ZODIAC GUIDE TO
TAURUS

THE ZODIAC GUIDE TO
GEMINI

THE ZODIAC GUIDE TO
CANCER

THE ZODIAC GUIDE TO
LEO

THE ZODIAC GUIDE TO
VIRGO

THE ZODIAC GUIDE TO
LIBRA

THE ZODIAC GUIDE TO
SCORPIO

THE ZODIAC GUIDE TO
SAGITTARIUS

THE ZODIAC GUIDE TO
CAPRICORN

THE ZODIAC GUIDE TO
AQUARIUS

THE ZODIAC GUIDE TO
PISCES

Based on the symbolism of the wheel,
Red Wheel offers books and divination decks
from a variety of traditions. We aim to provide the
ideas, information, and innovative approaches to
help you develop your own spiritual path.

Please visit our website, www.redwheelweiser.com,
to learn more about our full range of titles.